50 Classic Italian Pasta Dish Recipes for Home

By: Kelly Johnson

Table of Contents

- Orecchiette with Sausage and Broccoli
- Ravioli di Pesce
- Spaghetti al Limone
- Gemelli with Sausage and Peppers
- Pappardelle al Cinghiale
- Fettuccine al Tartufo
- Tortellini al Ragù
- Spaghetti alla Puttanesca
- Linguine with Tomato Cream Sauce
- Pasta alla Caprese
- Tagliatelle ai Funghi
- Lasagna with Bechamel
- Bucatini with Tomato Sauce
- Ravioli di Ricotta al Burro e Salvia
- Fettuccine alla Ricotta

Spaghetti Aglio e Olio

Ingredients:

- 400 g (14 oz) spaghetti
- 6 cloves garlic, thinly sliced
- 1/2 cup (120 ml) extra-virgin olive oil
- 1/2 tsp red pepper flakes (adjust to taste)
- Salt, to taste
- Freshly ground black pepper, to taste
- 1/4 cup (15 g) fresh parsley, chopped
- Grated Parmesan cheese (optional, for serving)

Instructions:

1. **Cook the Pasta**
   Bring a large pot of salted water to a boil. Add the spaghetti and cook according to the package instructions until al dente. Reserve about 1 cup of pasta cooking water, then drain the pasta.

2. **Prepare the Aglio e Olio Sauce**
   While the pasta is cooking, heat the olive oil in a large skillet over medium heat. Add the sliced garlic and sauté until it turns golden brown, being careful not to burn it (about 2-3 minutes). Add the red pepper flakes and sauté for an additional 30 seconds.

3. **Combine Pasta and Sauce**
   Add the drained spaghetti to the skillet with the garlic oil. Toss to combine, adding reserved pasta cooking water a little at a time until the desired consistency is reached. Season with salt and freshly ground black pepper to taste.

4. **Finish and Serve**
   Remove from heat and stir in the chopped parsley. Serve immediately, garnished with grated Parmesan cheese if desired. Enjoy your homemade Spaghetti Aglio e Olio!

Fettuccine Alfredo

Ingredients:

- 400 g (14 oz) fettuccine
- 1/2 cup (115 g) unsalted butter
- 1 cup (240 ml) heavy cream
- 1 1/2 cups (150 g) grated Parmesan cheese
- Salt and freshly ground black pepper, to taste
- Fresh parsley, chopped (for garnish)

Instructions:

1. **Cook the Pasta**
   Bring a large pot of salted water to a boil. Add the fettuccine and cook until al dente. Reserve 1 cup of pasta cooking water, then drain the pasta.
2. **Make the Sauce**
   In a large skillet, melt the butter over medium heat. Add the heavy cream and simmer for 2-3 minutes, stirring constantly.
3. **Combine Pasta and Sauce**
   Add the drained fettuccine to the skillet, along with the Parmesan cheese. Toss until the pasta is coated, adding reserved pasta water as needed to reach the desired consistency. Season with salt and pepper.
4. **Serve**
   Garnish with fresh parsley and additional Parmesan cheese if desired.

Penne Arrabbiata

Ingredients:

- 400 g (14 oz) penne pasta
- 3 tbsp olive oil
- 4 cloves garlic, minced
- 1/2 tsp red pepper flakes (adjust to taste)
- 1 can (400 g) crushed tomatoes
- Salt and pepper, to taste
- Fresh basil leaves, torn (for garnish)

Instructions:

1. **Cook the Pasta**
   Bring a large pot of salted water to a boil. Add the penne and cook until al dente.
2. **Make the Sauce**
   In a skillet, heat the olive oil over medium heat. Add the minced garlic and red pepper flakes, sautéing until fragrant (about 1 minute).
3. **Add Tomatoes**
   Add the crushed tomatoes, salt, and pepper. Simmer for about 10 minutes.
4. **Combine Pasta and Sauce**
   Drain the pasta and add it to the sauce, tossing to combine.
5. **Serve**
   Garnish with fresh basil leaves before serving.

Lasagna Bolognese

Ingredients:

- 12 lasagna noodles
- 2 cups (500 g) Bolognese sauce
- 2 cups (500 g) ricotta cheese
- 2 cups (200 g) shredded mozzarella cheese
- 1/2 cup (50 g) grated Parmesan cheese
- 1 egg
- Salt and pepper, to taste
- Fresh basil (for garnish)

Instructions:

1. **Preheat the Oven**
   Preheat your oven to 180°C (350°F).
2. **Prepare Ricotta Mixture**
   In a bowl, mix ricotta cheese, egg, salt, and pepper.
3. **Assemble the Lasagna**
   Spread a layer of Bolognese sauce in a baking dish. Layer 4 lasagna noodles, half the ricotta mixture, half the mozzarella, and more Bolognese sauce. Repeat, finishing with noodles and remaining Bolognese sauce. Top with mozzarella and Parmesan.
4. **Bake**
   Cover with foil and bake for 25 minutes. Remove the foil and bake for another 15-20 minutes until golden and bubbly.
5. **Serve**
   Let cool for a few minutes, then garnish with fresh basil before serving.

Tagliatelle al Ragu

Ingredients:

- 400 g (14 oz) tagliatelle
- 2 tbsp olive oil
- 1 onion, chopped
- 2 carrots, chopped
- 2 celery stalks, chopped
- 400 g (14 oz) ground beef
- 1 can (400 g) crushed tomatoes
- 1 cup (240 ml) red wine
- Salt and pepper, to taste
- Grated Parmesan cheese (for serving)

Instructions:

1. **Cook the Pasta**
   Bring a large pot of salted water to a boil. Cook the tagliatelle until al dente, then drain.
2. **Make the Ragu**
   In a large skillet, heat the olive oil over medium heat. Add the onion, carrots, and celery, cooking until softened. Add the ground beef and cook until browned.
3. **Add Tomatoes and Wine**
   Stir in the crushed tomatoes and red wine. Simmer for about 30 minutes, seasoning with salt and pepper.
4. **Combine Pasta and Ragu**
   Add the drained tagliatelle to the sauce, tossing to coat.
5. **Serve**
   Serve hot, garnished with grated Parmesan cheese.

Spaghetti Carbonara

Ingredients:

- 400 g (14 oz) spaghetti
- 150 g (5 oz) pancetta or guanciale, diced
- 3 large eggs
- 1 cup (100 g) grated Pecorino Romano cheese
- Salt and freshly ground black pepper, to taste
- Fresh parsley, chopped (for garnish)

Instructions:

1. **Cook the Pasta**
   Bring a large pot of salted water to a boil. Add the spaghetti and cook until al dente.
2. **Cook Pancetta**
   In a large skillet, cook the pancetta over medium heat until crispy. Remove from heat.
3. **Make the Sauce**
   In a bowl, whisk together the eggs and Pecorino Romano cheese, adding salt and pepper.
4. **Combine Pasta and Sauce**
   Drain the spaghetti, reserving some pasta water. Quickly add the pasta to the skillet with pancetta, then remove from heat. Stir in the egg mixture, adding reserved pasta water as needed to create a creamy sauce.
5. **Serve**
   Garnish with parsley and additional cheese if desired.

Linguine alle Vongole

Ingredients:

- 400 g (14 oz) linguine
- 2 tbsp olive oil
- 4 cloves garlic, minced
- 1/2 tsp red pepper flakes (optional)
- 1 cup (240 ml) white wine
- 1 kg (2 lbs) fresh clams, scrubbed
- Fresh parsley, chopped (for garnish)
- Salt and pepper, to taste

Instructions:

1. **Cook the Pasta**
   Bring a large pot of salted water to a boil. Cook the linguine until al dente.
2. **Prepare the Sauce**
   In a large skillet, heat the olive oil over medium heat. Add the garlic and red pepper flakes, cooking until fragrant.
3. **Add Wine and Clams**
   Pour in the white wine, bring to a boil, and then add the clams. Cover and cook until the clams open, about 5-7 minutes. Discard any unopened clams.
4. **Combine Pasta and Sauce**
   Add the drained linguine to the skillet and toss to combine.
5. **Serve**
   Garnish with fresh parsley before serving.

Pesto Genovese with Trofie

Ingredients:

- 400 g (14 oz) trofie pasta
- 2 cups fresh basil leaves
- 1/2 cup (120 ml) extra-virgin olive oil
- 1/2 cup (50 g) grated Parmesan cheese
- 1/4 cup (30 g) pine nuts, toasted
- 2 cloves garlic
- Salt, to taste

Instructions:

1. **Cook the Pasta**
   Bring a large pot of salted water to a boil. Cook the trofie until al dente.
2. **Make the Pesto**
   In a food processor, combine the basil, garlic, pine nuts, and Parmesan. Blend while slowly adding the olive oil until smooth. Season with salt.
3. **Combine Pasta and Pesto**
   Drain the trofie and add it to the pesto, tossing to coat evenly.
4. **Serve**
   Serve immediately, garnished with additional Parmesan if desired.

Ravioli di Ricotta e Spinaci

Ingredients:

- 400 g (14 oz) fresh pasta (ravioli)
- 250 g (9 oz) ricotta cheese
- 200 g (7 oz) spinach, cooked and chopped
- 1/2 cup (50 g) grated Parmesan cheese
- 1 egg
- Salt and pepper, to taste
- 1/4 cup (60 g) butter
- Fresh sage leaves (for garnish)

Instructions:

1. **Prepare the Filling**
   In a bowl, mix together ricotta, spinach, Parmesan, egg, salt, and pepper.
2. **Fill the Ravioli**
   Lay out the pasta sheets and place spoonfuls of the filling on one half. Fold over and seal the edges.
3. **Cook the Ravioli**
   Bring a large pot of salted water to a boil. Cook the ravioli until they float (about 3-4 minutes).
4. **Make the Sauce**
   In a skillet, melt butter over medium heat and add sage leaves, cooking until fragrant.
5. **Serve**
   Drain the ravioli and toss in the butter sauce. Serve hot, garnished with more Parmesan.

Orecchiette with Broccoli Rabe

Ingredients:

- 400 g (14 oz) orecchiette pasta
- 400 g (14 oz) broccoli rabe, trimmed and chopped
- 3 tbsp olive oil
- 3 cloves garlic, minced
- 1/2 tsp red pepper flakes (optional)
- Salt and pepper, to taste
- Grated Parmesan cheese (for serving)

Instructions:

1. **Cook the Pasta**
   Bring a large pot of salted water to a boil. Add the orecchiette and cook until al dente, adding the broccoli rabe for the last 2-3 minutes.
2. **Prepare the Sauce**
   In a skillet, heat olive oil over medium heat. Add garlic and red pepper flakes, sautéing until fragrant.
3. **Combine Pasta and Sauce**
   Drain the pasta and broccoli rabe, then add to the skillet. Toss to coat in the oil and garlic.
4. **Serve**
   Season with salt and pepper, and serve with grated Parmesan cheese.

Fettuccine al Pesto

Ingredients:

- 400 g (14 oz) fettuccine
- 2 cups fresh basil leaves
- 1/2 cup (120 ml) extra-virgin olive oil
- 1/2 cup (50 g) grated Parmesan cheese
- 1/4 cup (30 g) pine nuts, toasted
- 2 cloves garlic
- Salt, to taste

Instructions:

1. **Cook the Pasta**
   Bring a large pot of salted water to a boil. Cook the fettuccine until al dente.
2. **Make the Pesto**
   In a food processor, combine basil, garlic, pine nuts, and Parmesan. Blend while slowly adding olive oil until smooth. Season with salt.
3. **Combine Pasta and Pesto**
   Drain the fettuccine and add to the pesto, tossing to coat.
4. **Serve**
   Serve immediately, garnished with additional Parmesan if desired.

Pasta Primavera

Ingredients:

- 400 g (14 oz) pasta (your choice)
- 2 tbsp olive oil
- 1 zucchini, sliced
- 1 bell pepper, sliced
- 1 cup (150 g) cherry tomatoes, halved
- 1 cup (150 g) asparagus, trimmed and cut into pieces
- 2 cloves garlic, minced
- Salt and pepper, to taste
- Fresh basil, chopped (for garnish)
- Grated Parmesan cheese (for serving)

Instructions:

1. **Cook the Pasta**
   Bring a large pot of salted water to a boil. Cook the pasta until al dente.
2. **Sauté the Vegetables**
   In a large skillet, heat olive oil over medium heat. Add zucchini, bell pepper, asparagus, and garlic, sautéing until tender.
3. **Combine Pasta and Vegetables**
   Drain the pasta and add it to the skillet, tossing to combine. Add cherry tomatoes and cook for another minute.
4. **Serve**
   Season with salt and pepper, garnish with fresh basil and Parmesan cheese before serving.

Cannelloni Ricotta e Spinaci

Ingredients:

- 12 cannelloni tubes
- 250 g (9 oz) ricotta cheese
- 200 g (7 oz) spinach, cooked and chopped
- 2 cups (500 ml) marinara sauce
- 1 cup (100 g) grated mozzarella cheese
- 1/2 cup (50 g) grated Parmesan cheese
- 1 egg
- Salt and pepper, to taste

Instructions:

1. **Preheat the Oven**
   Preheat your oven to 180°C (350°F).
2. **Prepare the Filling**
   In a bowl, mix ricotta, spinach, egg, salt, and pepper.
3. **Fill the Cannelloni**
   Stuff each cannelloni tube with the filling.
4. **Assemble**
   Spread a layer of marinara sauce in a baking dish. Arrange the filled cannelloni on top and cover with remaining sauce.
5. **Top and Bake**
   Sprinkle with mozzarella and Parmesan cheese. Cover with foil and bake for 25 minutes. Remove the foil and bake for an additional 15 minutes until golden and bubbly.

Spaghetti al Pomodoro

Ingredients:

- 400 g (14 oz) spaghetti
- 3 tbsp olive oil
- 4 cloves garlic, minced
- 1 can (400 g) crushed tomatoes
- Salt and pepper, to taste
- Fresh basil leaves (for garnish)
- Grated Parmesan cheese (for serving)

Instructions:

1. **Cook the Pasta**
   Bring a large pot of salted water to a boil. Cook the spaghetti until al dente.
2. **Make the Sauce**
   In a skillet, heat olive oil over medium heat. Add garlic and sauté until fragrant. Add crushed tomatoes, salt, and pepper. Simmer for about 10-15 minutes.
3. **Combine Pasta and Sauce**
   Drain the spaghetti and add it to the sauce, tossing to combine.
4. **Serve**
   Garnish with fresh basil leaves and serve with grated Parmesan cheese.

Tortellini in Brodo

Ingredients:

- 400 g (14 oz) tortellini (fresh or dried)
- 1.5 liters (6 cups) chicken or vegetable broth
- 1 carrot, diced
- 1 celery stalk, diced
- 1 onion, diced
- Salt and pepper, to taste
- Fresh parsley, chopped (for garnish)

Instructions:

1. **Prepare the Broth**
   In a large pot, bring the broth to a simmer. Add diced carrot, celery, and onion, cooking until vegetables are tender.
2. **Cook the Tortellini**
   Add the tortellini to the broth and cook according to package instructions until they float (about 2-3 minutes for fresh, longer for dried).
3. **Serve**
   Season with salt and pepper. Serve hot, garnished with fresh parsley.

Gnocchi di Patate al Pesto

Ingredients:

- 1 kg (2.2 lbs) potatoes
- 300 g (10.5 oz) all-purpose flour
- 1 egg
- Salt, to taste
- 2 cups fresh basil leaves
- 1/2 cup (120 ml) extra-virgin olive oil
- 1/2 cup (50 g) grated Parmesan cheese
- 1/4 cup (30 g) pine nuts, toasted
- 2 cloves garlic
- Grated Parmesan cheese (for serving)

Instructions:

1. **Prepare the Gnocchi**
   Boil the potatoes until tender. Peel and mash them while still warm. In a bowl, mix mashed potatoes, flour, egg, and salt until a dough forms.
2. **Shape the Gnocchi**
   Roll the dough into long ropes and cut into small pieces. Use a fork to create ridges.
3. **Cook the Gnocchi**
   Boil a pot of salted water. Add the gnocchi and cook until they float (about 2-3 minutes).
4. **Make the Pesto**
   In a food processor, combine basil, garlic, pine nuts, and Parmesan. Blend while adding olive oil until smooth.
5. **Combine and Serve**
   Toss the gnocchi in pesto sauce and serve with additional Parmesan cheese.

Pasta e Fagioli

Ingredients:

- 250 g (9 oz) small pasta (like ditalini)
- 400 g (14 oz) canned cannellini beans, drained and rinsed
- 1 onion, chopped
- 2 carrots, diced
- 2 celery stalks, diced
- 2 cloves garlic, minced
- 1 can (400 g) crushed tomatoes
- 4 cups (1 liter) vegetable broth
- Olive oil, salt, and pepper, to taste
- Fresh parsley, chopped (for garnish)

Instructions:

1. **Sauté the Vegetables**
   In a large pot, heat olive oil over medium heat. Add onion, carrots, celery, and garlic, cooking until softened.
2. **Add Tomatoes and Broth**
   Stir in crushed tomatoes and vegetable broth. Bring to a boil.
3. **Cook the Pasta**
   Add the pasta and cook until al dente. Stir in cannellini beans.
4. **Serve**
   Season with salt and pepper, and serve hot, garnished with fresh parsley.

Farfalle al Salmone

Ingredients:

- 400 g (14 oz) farfalle pasta
- 200 g (7 oz) smoked salmon, sliced
- 1 cup (250 ml) heavy cream
- 1/2 cup (50 g) grated Parmesan cheese
- 1/2 lemon, juiced
- Salt and pepper, to taste
- Fresh dill, for garnish

Instructions:

1. **Cook the Pasta**
   Bring a large pot of salted water to a boil. Cook farfalle until al dente.
2. **Prepare the Sauce**
   In a skillet, heat the cream over medium heat. Add lemon juice, salt, and pepper. Stir in the salmon and Parmesan.
3. **Combine Pasta and Sauce**
   Drain the pasta and add it to the skillet, tossing to coat.
4. **Serve**
   Garnish with fresh dill before serving.

Lasagna Verde

Ingredients:

- 12 sheets of lasagna noodles
- 400 g (14 oz) spinach, cooked and chopped
- 250 g (9 oz) ricotta cheese
- 2 cups (500 ml) béchamel sauce
- 1 cup (100 g) grated Parmesan cheese
- Salt and pepper, to taste
- 2 cups (500 g) marinara sauce

Instructions:

1. **Preheat the Oven**
   Preheat your oven to 180°C (350°F).
2. **Prepare the Filling**
   In a bowl, mix cooked spinach, ricotta, salt, and pepper.
3. **Layer the Lasagna**
   In a baking dish, spread a layer of marinara sauce. Layer with lasagna noodles, spinach filling, béchamel, and Parmesan. Repeat the layers.
4. **Bake**
   Top with remaining marinara and cheese. Cover with foil and bake for 30 minutes. Remove foil and bake for an additional 15 minutes until golden.

Bucatini all'Amatriciana

Ingredients:

- 400 g (14 oz) bucatini pasta
- 150 g (5 oz) guanciale or pancetta, diced
- 1 can (400 g) crushed tomatoes
- 1/2 cup (50 g) grated Pecorino Romano cheese
- 1/2 tsp red pepper flakes (optional)
- Salt and pepper, to taste
- Fresh basil, for garnish

Instructions:

1. **Cook the Pasta**
   Bring a large pot of salted water to a boil. Cook bucatini until al dente.
2. **Prepare the Sauce**
   In a skillet, cook the guanciale over medium heat until crispy. Add crushed tomatoes, red pepper flakes, salt, and pepper. Simmer for 10 minutes.
3. **Combine Pasta and Sauce**
   Drain the pasta and add it to the skillet, tossing to coat.
4. **Serve**
   Garnish with Pecorino Romano and fresh basil before serving.

Spaghetti alle Noci

Ingredients:

- 400 g (14 oz) spaghetti
- 200 g (7 oz) walnuts, chopped
- 3 cloves garlic, minced
- 1/2 cup (120 ml) extra-virgin olive oil
- Salt and pepper, to taste
- Fresh parsley, chopped (for garnish)
- Grated Parmesan cheese (for serving)

Instructions:

1. **Cook the Pasta**
   Bring a large pot of salted water to a boil. Cook spaghetti until al dente.
2. **Prepare the Sauce**
   In a skillet, heat olive oil over medium heat. Add garlic and walnuts, cooking until fragrant.
3. **Combine Pasta and Sauce**
   Drain the spaghetti and add it to the skillet, tossing to combine.
4. **Serve**
   Season with salt and pepper, and serve garnished with fresh parsley and Parmesan cheese.

Maccheroni al Formaggio

Ingredients:

- 400 g (14 oz) elbow macaroni
- 4 cups (1 liter) milk
- 1/4 cup (60 g) butter
- 1/4 cup (30 g) all-purpose flour
- 2 cups (200 g) shredded cheddar cheese
- Salt and pepper, to taste
- Bread crumbs (for topping)

Instructions:

1. **Cook the Pasta**
   Bring a large pot of salted water to a boil. Cook macaroni until al dente. Drain and set aside.
2. **Make the Cheese Sauce**
   In a saucepan, melt butter over medium heat. Whisk in flour, cooking for 1 minute. Gradually add milk, whisking until thickened. Stir in cheese until melted.
3. **Combine Pasta and Sauce**
   Mix macaroni with cheese sauce. Pour into a baking dish and sprinkle with bread crumbs.
4. **Bake**
   Preheat the oven to 180°C (350°F). Bake for 20-25 minutes until bubbly and golden on top.

Lasagna di Verdure

Ingredients:

- 12 lasagna sheets
- 2 cups assorted vegetables (zucchini, eggplant, bell peppers, etc.), roasted
- 2 cups ricotta cheese
- 2 cups marinara sauce
- 2 cups béchamel sauce
- 1 cup grated Parmesan cheese
- Salt and pepper, to taste
- Fresh basil leaves, for garnish

Instructions:

1. **Preheat the Oven**
   Preheat your oven to 180°C (350°F).
2. **Layer the Lasagna**
   In a baking dish, spread a layer of marinara sauce. Layer with lasagna sheets, roasted vegetables, ricotta, béchamel, and Parmesan. Repeat the layers.
3. **Top and Bake**
   Finish with a layer of béchamel and Parmesan. Cover with foil and bake for 30 minutes. Remove foil and bake for an additional 15 minutes until golden.
4. **Serve**
   Let it cool slightly before serving, garnished with fresh basil leaves.

Penne al Forno

Ingredients:

- 400 g (14 oz) penne pasta
- 2 cups marinara sauce
- 1 cup ricotta cheese
- 1 cup mozzarella cheese, shredded
- 1/2 cup grated Parmesan cheese
- 1 tsp dried oregano
- Salt and pepper, to taste
- Fresh basil, for garnish

Instructions:

1. **Cook the Pasta**
   Bring a large pot of salted water to a boil. Cook penne until al dente.
2. **Mix Ingredients**
   In a large bowl, combine cooked penne, marinara sauce, ricotta, oregano, salt, and pepper.
3. **Layer and Bake**
   Transfer the mixture to a baking dish. Top with mozzarella and Parmesan. Bake at 180°C (350°F) for 25-30 minutes until bubbly and golden.
4. **Serve**
   Garnish with fresh basil before serving.

Ravioli di Carne

Ingredients:

- 400 g (14 oz) fresh pasta sheets
- 300 g (10.5 oz) ground beef
- 100 g (3.5 oz) ground pork
- 1/2 onion, finely chopped
- 1 clove garlic, minced
- 1 egg
- 1/2 cup grated Parmesan cheese
- Salt and pepper, to taste
- Marinara sauce, for serving

Instructions:

1. **Prepare the Filling**
   In a skillet, sauté onion and garlic until soft. Add beef and pork, cooking until browned. Mix in egg, Parmesan, salt, and pepper.
2. **Assemble the Ravioli**
   Place spoonfuls of filling on pasta sheets, fold, and seal edges.
3. **Cook the Ravioli**
   Boil a pot of salted water. Cook ravioli until they float (about 3-4 minutes).
4. **Serve**
   Drain and serve with marinara sauce.

Spaghetti con le Sarde

Ingredients:

- 400 g (14 oz) spaghetti
- 200 g (7 oz) sardines, cleaned and filleted
- 1 onion, thinly sliced
- 2 cloves garlic, minced
- 1/4 cup olive oil
- 1/2 cup bread crumbs
- 1/4 cup raisins
- 1/4 cup pine nuts
- Salt and pepper, to taste
- Fresh parsley, chopped (for garnish)

Instructions:

1. **Cook the Pasta**
   Bring a large pot of salted water to a boil. Cook spaghetti until al dente.
2. **Prepare the Sauce**
   In a skillet, heat olive oil. Sauté onion and garlic until soft. Add sardines, raisins, and pine nuts, cooking gently.
3. **Combine Pasta and Sauce**
   Drain the pasta and add it to the skillet, tossing to coat.
4. **Serve**
   Top with bread crumbs and garnish with parsley before serving.

Ziti alla Genovese

Ingredients:

- 400 g (14 oz) ziti pasta
- 500 g (1.1 lbs) beef chuck, diced
- 2 onions, sliced
- 2 carrots, diced
- 2 celery stalks, diced
- 1 cup white wine
- 2 cups beef broth
- Salt and pepper, to taste
- Fresh basil, for garnish

Instructions:

1. **Sauté the Vegetables**
   In a pot, sauté onions, carrots, and celery in olive oil until soft.
2. **Cook the Beef**
   Add beef and brown on all sides. Pour in wine and simmer until evaporated.
3. **Add Broth and Cook**
   Add broth, salt, and pepper. Simmer for about 1.5 hours until tender.
4. **Cook the Pasta**
   Meanwhile, cook ziti until al dente. Combine with the meat sauce and serve garnished with fresh basil.

Fettuccine alla Bolognese

Ingredients:

- 400 g (14 oz) fettuccine pasta
- 300 g (10.5 oz) ground beef
- 100 g (3.5 oz) ground pork
- 1 onion, finely chopped
- 1 carrot, finely chopped
- 1 celery stalk, finely chopped
- 1 can (400 g) crushed tomatoes
- 1 cup red wine
- 1 cup milk
- Olive oil, salt, and pepper, to taste
- Grated Parmesan cheese, for serving

Instructions:

1. **Sauté the Vegetables**
   In a large pot, heat olive oil. Add onion, carrot, and celery, cooking until soft.
2. **Brown the Meat**
   Add ground beef and pork, cooking until browned.
3. **Add Wine and Tomatoes**
   Pour in wine and simmer until evaporated. Add crushed tomatoes and milk. Cook on low heat for about 1.5 hours.
4. **Cook the Pasta**
   Boil fettuccine until al dente. Combine with the sauce and serve with grated Parmesan.

Spaghetti Cacio e Pepe

Ingredients:

- 400 g (14 oz) spaghetti
- 100 g (3.5 oz) Pecorino Romano cheese, grated
- Freshly cracked black pepper, to taste
- Salt, to taste

Instructions:

1. **Cook the Pasta**
   Bring a large pot of salted water to a boil. Cook spaghetti until al dente.
2. **Prepare the Sauce**
   In a bowl, combine Pecorino Romano and black pepper.
3. **Combine Pasta and Sauce**
   Reserve some pasta water and drain the spaghetti. Add it to the bowl with cheese and pepper, mixing quickly while adding reserved pasta water to create a creamy sauce.
4. **Serve**
   Serve immediately with extra cheese and pepper on top.

Fusilli al Pomodoro

Ingredients:

- 400 g (14 oz) fusilli pasta
- 2 cups ripe tomatoes, chopped
- 2 cloves garlic, minced
- 1/4 cup olive oil
- Salt and pepper, to taste
- Fresh basil leaves, for garnish
- Grated Parmesan cheese, for serving

Instructions:

1. **Cook the Pasta**
   Bring a large pot of salted water to a boil. Cook fusilli until al dente.
2. **Prepare the Sauce**
   In a skillet, heat olive oil over medium heat. Add garlic and sauté until fragrant.
   Add tomatoes, salt, and pepper. Simmer for 10 minutes.
3. **Combine Pasta and Sauce**
   Drain the pasta and add it to the skillet. Toss to combine.
4. **Serve**
   Garnish with fresh basil and grated Parmesan before serving.

Tortellini alla Panna

Ingredients:

- 400 g (14 oz) tortellini (fresh or dried)
- 1 cup heavy cream
- 1/2 cup grated Parmesan cheese
- 2 tbsp butter
- Salt and pepper, to taste
- Fresh parsley, for garnish

Instructions:

1. **Cook the Tortellini**
   Boil a pot of salted water and cook tortellini according to package instructions.
2. **Prepare the Sauce**
   In a skillet, melt butter over medium heat. Add cream and bring to a simmer. Stir in Parmesan, salt, and pepper.
3. **Combine Tortellini and Sauce**
   Drain tortellini and add to the sauce. Toss to coat evenly.
4. **Serve**
   Garnish with fresh parsley and additional Parmesan.

Linguine al Limone

Ingredients:

- 400 g (14 oz) linguine pasta
- 1/4 cup olive oil
- Zest and juice of 2 lemons
- 1/2 cup grated Parmesan cheese
- Salt and pepper, to taste
- Fresh parsley, for garnish

Instructions:

1. **Cook the Pasta**
   Bring a large pot of salted water to a boil. Cook linguine until al dente.
2. **Prepare the Sauce**
   In a bowl, whisk together olive oil, lemon zest, juice, salt, and pepper.
3. **Combine Pasta and Sauce**
   Drain linguine and toss it with the lemon sauce. Stir in Parmesan.
4. **Serve**
   Garnish with fresh parsley before serving.

Spaghetti al Nero di Seppia

Ingredients:

- 400 g (14 oz) spaghetti
- 200 g (7 oz) cuttlefish or squid, cleaned and cut into strips
- 2 cloves garlic, minced
- 1/4 cup olive oil
- 1/4 cup white wine
- 2 tbsp squid ink
- Salt and pepper, to taste
- Fresh parsley, for garnish

Instructions:

1. **Cook the Pasta**
   Boil salted water and cook spaghetti until al dente.
2. **Prepare the Sauce**
   In a skillet, heat olive oil over medium heat. Add garlic and sauté until fragrant. Add cuttlefish and cook until opaque.
3. **Add Wine and Ink**
   Pour in wine and let it evaporate. Stir in squid ink, salt, and pepper.
4. **Combine Pasta and Sauce**
   Drain spaghetti and add it to the skillet, tossing to combine.
5. **Serve**
   Garnish with fresh parsley before serving.

Capellini Aglio e Olio

Ingredients:

- 400 g (14 oz) capellini (angel hair) pasta
- 4 cloves garlic, thinly sliced
- 1/2 cup olive oil
- 1/4 tsp red pepper flakes (optional)
- Salt and pepper, to taste
- Fresh parsley, chopped, for garnish
- Grated Parmesan cheese, for serving

Instructions:

1. **Cook the Pasta**
   Bring a large pot of salted water to a boil. Cook capellini until al dente.
2. **Prepare the Sauce**
   In a skillet, heat olive oil over medium heat. Add garlic and sauté until golden. Add red pepper flakes, salt, and pepper.
3. **Combine Pasta and Sauce**
   Drain the pasta and add it to the skillet, tossing to coat.
4. **Serve**
   Garnish with fresh parsley and Parmesan before serving.

Farfalle al Pesto Rosso

Ingredients:

- 400 g (14 oz) farfalle pasta
- 1 cup sun-dried tomatoes, drained and chopped
- 1/2 cup almonds
- 1/2 cup grated Parmesan cheese
- 1/2 cup olive oil
- 1 clove garlic
- Salt and pepper, to taste
- Fresh basil, for garnish

Instructions:

1. **Cook the Pasta**
   Bring a large pot of salted water to a boil. Cook farfalle until al dente.
2. **Prepare the Pesto**
   In a food processor, combine sun-dried tomatoes, almonds, Parmesan, olive oil, garlic, salt, and pepper. Blend until smooth.
3. **Combine Pasta and Pesto**
   Drain pasta and toss it with the pesto until well coated.
4. **Serve**
   Garnish with fresh basil before serving.

Orecchiette with Sausage and Broccoli

Ingredients:

- 400 g (14 oz) orecchiette pasta
- 300 g (10.5 oz) Italian sausage, casings removed
- 2 cups broccoli florets
- 2 cloves garlic, minced
- 1/4 cup olive oil
- Salt and pepper, to taste
- Grated Parmesan cheese, for serving

Instructions:

1. **Cook the Pasta**
   Boil a pot of salted water and cook orecchiette until al dente. Add broccoli florets in the last 3-4 minutes of cooking.
2. **Cook the Sausage**
   In a skillet, heat olive oil over medium heat. Add sausage and cook until browned. Add garlic and cook until fragrant.
3. **Combine Pasta and Sausage**
   Drain the pasta and broccoli, then toss them with the sausage mixture.
4. **Serve**
   Season with salt and pepper, and serve with grated Parmesan.

Ravioli di Pesce

Ingredients:

- 400 g (14 oz) fish ravioli (store-bought or homemade)
- 1 cup seafood stock
- 1/2 cup heavy cream
- 2 cloves garlic, minced
- 1/4 cup olive oil
- Salt and pepper, to taste
- Fresh parsley, for garnish

Instructions:

1. **Cook the Ravioli**
   Boil salted water and cook the fish ravioli according to package instructions.
2. **Prepare the Sauce**
   In a skillet, heat olive oil over medium heat. Add garlic and sauté until fragrant. Add seafood stock and bring to a simmer. Stir in heavy cream, salt, and pepper.
3. **Combine Ravioli and Sauce**
   Drain the ravioli and add them to the skillet, tossing to coat evenly.
4. **Serve**
   Garnish with fresh parsley before serving.

Spaghetti al Limone

Ingredients:

- 400 g (14 oz) spaghetti
- 1/4 cup olive oil
- Zest and juice of 2 lemons
- 1/2 cup grated Parmesan cheese
- Salt and pepper, to taste
- Fresh parsley, for garnish

Instructions:

1. **Cook the Pasta**
   Boil a large pot of salted water and cook spaghetti until al dente.
2. **Prepare the Sauce**
   In a bowl, whisk together olive oil, lemon zest, lemon juice, salt, and pepper.
3. **Combine Pasta and Sauce**
   Drain spaghetti and toss it with the lemon sauce. Stir in Parmesan cheese.
4. **Serve**
   Garnish with fresh parsley before serving.

Gemelli with Sausage and Peppers

Ingredients:

- 400 g (14 oz) gemelli pasta
- 300 g (10.5 oz) Italian sausage, casings removed
- 1 bell pepper, sliced
- 1 onion, sliced
- 2 cloves garlic, minced
- 1/4 cup olive oil
- Salt and pepper, to taste
- Fresh basil, for garnish

Instructions:

1. **Cook the Pasta**
   Boil salted water and cook gemelli until al dente.
2. **Cook the Sausage**
   In a skillet, heat olive oil over medium heat. Add sausage and cook until browned.
3. **Add Peppers and Onions**
   Add bell pepper, onion, and garlic to the skillet. Cook until vegetables are tender.
4. **Combine Pasta and Sauce**
   Drain the pasta and toss it with the sausage and pepper mixture.
5. **Serve**
   Season with salt and pepper and garnish with fresh basil.

Pappardelle al Cinghiale

Ingredients:

- 400 g (14 oz) pappardelle pasta
- 500 g (1 lb) wild boar meat, diced
- 1 onion, chopped
- 2 cloves garlic, minced
- 1 cup red wine
- 1 cup crushed tomatoes
- 1/4 cup olive oil
- Salt and pepper, to taste
- Fresh rosemary, for garnish

Instructions:

1. **Cook the Pasta**
   Boil salted water and cook pappardelle until al dente.
2. **Cook the Meat**
   In a large skillet, heat olive oil over medium heat. Add onion and garlic, sauté until softened. Add wild boar meat and brown on all sides.
3. **Add Wine and Tomatoes**
   Pour in red wine and let it reduce. Add crushed tomatoes, salt, and pepper, and simmer for 30-40 minutes.
4. **Combine Pasta and Sauce**
   Drain the pasta and toss it with the wild boar sauce.
5. **Serve**
   Garnish with fresh rosemary before serving.

Fettuccine al Tartufo

Ingredients:

- 400 g (14 oz) fettuccine pasta
- 1/2 cup heavy cream
- 1/4 cup truffle oil
- 1/2 cup grated Parmesan cheese
- Salt and pepper, to taste
- Fresh truffles or truffle shavings, for garnish

Instructions:

1. **Cook the Pasta**
   Boil a large pot of salted water and cook fettuccine until al dente.
2. **Prepare the Sauce**
   In a skillet, heat heavy cream over medium heat. Stir in truffle oil, salt, and pepper.
3. **Combine Pasta and Sauce**
   Drain fettuccine and toss it with the truffle sauce and Parmesan.
4. **Serve**
   Garnish with fresh truffles or truffle shavings before serving.

Tortellini al Ragù

Ingredients:

- 400 g (14 oz) tortellini (fresh or dried)
- 2 cups meat ragù (prepared or store-bought)
- 1/4 cup grated Parmesan cheese
- Salt and pepper, to taste
- Fresh basil, for garnish

Instructions:

1. **Cook the Tortellini**
   Boil salted water and cook tortellini according to package instructions.
2. **Heat the Ragù**
   In a saucepan, heat the meat ragù over medium heat until warmed through.
3. **Combine Tortellini and Ragù**
   Drain tortellini and toss them with the ragù.
4. **Serve**
   Season with salt and pepper, and garnish with grated Parmesan and fresh basil.

Spaghetti alla Puttanesca

Ingredients:

- 400 g (14 oz) spaghetti
- 4 cloves garlic, minced
- 1/2 cup black olives, pitted and sliced
- 2 tbsp capers
- 1 can (400 g) crushed tomatoes
- 1/4 cup olive oil
- Red pepper flakes, to taste
- Fresh parsley, for garnish

Instructions:

1. **Cook the Pasta**
   Boil salted water and cook spaghetti until al dente.
2. **Prepare the Sauce**
   In a skillet, heat olive oil over medium heat. Add garlic and sauté until fragrant. Stir in olives, capers, crushed tomatoes, and red pepper flakes. Simmer for 10-15 minutes.
3. **Combine Pasta and Sauce**
   Drain spaghetti and toss it with the sauce until well coated.
4. **Serve**
   Garnish with fresh parsley before serving.

Linguine with Tomato Cream Sauce

Ingredients:

- 400 g (14 oz) linguine
- 1 can (400 g) crushed tomatoes
- 1 cup heavy cream
- 2 cloves garlic, minced
- 1/4 cup olive oil
- Salt and pepper, to taste
- Fresh basil, for garnish

Instructions:

1. **Cook the Pasta**
   Boil a large pot of salted water and cook linguine until al dente.
2. **Prepare the Sauce**
   In a skillet, heat olive oil over medium heat. Add garlic and sauté until fragrant. Stir in crushed tomatoes and simmer for 10 minutes. Add heavy cream, salt, and pepper.
3. **Combine Pasta and Sauce**
   Drain linguine and toss it with the tomato cream sauce.
4. **Serve**
   Garnish with fresh basil before serving.

Pasta alla Caprese

Ingredients:

- 400 g (14 oz) pasta (penne or fusilli)
- 2 cups cherry tomatoes, halved
- 1 cup fresh mozzarella, cubed
- 1/4 cup fresh basil, chopped
- 1/4 cup olive oil
- Salt and pepper, to taste

Instructions:

1. **Cook the Pasta**
   Boil salted water and cook pasta until al dente.
2. **Combine Ingredients**
   In a large bowl, mix cherry tomatoes, mozzarella, basil, olive oil, salt, and pepper.
3. **Toss with Pasta**
   Drain pasta and add it to the bowl, tossing to combine.
4. **Serve**
   Serve immediately at room temperature.

Tagliatelle ai Funghi

Ingredients:

- 400 g (14 oz) tagliatelle
- 400 g (14 oz) mixed mushrooms, sliced
- 2 cloves garlic, minced
- 1/4 cup olive oil
- 1/2 cup heavy cream
- Salt and pepper, to taste
- Fresh parsley, for garnish

Instructions:

1. **Cook the Pasta**
   Boil a large pot of salted water and cook tagliatelle until al dente.
2. **Sauté the Mushrooms**
   In a skillet, heat olive oil over medium heat. Add garlic and sauté until fragrant. Add mushrooms and cook until browned.
3. **Prepare the Sauce**
   Stir in heavy cream, salt, and pepper, and simmer for a few minutes.
4. **Combine Pasta and Sauce**
   Drain the pasta and toss it with the mushroom sauce.
5. **Serve**
   Garnish with fresh parsley before serving.

Lasagna with Bechamel

Ingredients:

- 12 lasagna noodles
- 2 cups ricotta cheese
- 2 cups shredded mozzarella cheese
- 2 cups marinara sauce
- 1 cup bechamel sauce (butter, flour, milk)
- Salt and pepper, to taste
- Grated Parmesan cheese, for topping

Instructions:

1. **Prepare the Bechamel**
   In a saucepan, melt butter, add flour, and cook for 1 minute. Gradually whisk in milk and cook until thickened. Season with salt and pepper.
2. **Layer the Lasagna**
   In a baking dish, layer noodles, ricotta, marinara, bechamel, and mozzarella. Repeat until all ingredients are used.
3. **Top and Bake**
   Finish with bechamel and a sprinkle of Parmesan. Bake at 180°C (350°F) for 30-40 minutes until golden.
4. **Serve**
   Let cool for a few minutes before slicing.

Bucatini with Tomato Sauce

Ingredients:

- 400 g (14 oz) bucatini pasta
- 1 can (400 g) crushed tomatoes
- 2 cloves garlic, minced
- 1/4 cup olive oil
- Salt and pepper, to taste
- Fresh basil, for garnish

Instructions:

1. **Cook the Pasta**
   Boil a large pot of salted water and cook bucatini until al dente.
2. **Prepare the Sauce**
   In a skillet, heat olive oil over medium heat. Add garlic and sauté until fragrant. Stir in crushed tomatoes, salt, and pepper, and simmer for 15 minutes.
3. **Combine Pasta and Sauce**
   Drain bucatini and toss with the tomato sauce.
4. **Serve**
   Garnish with fresh basil before serving.

Ravioli di Ricotta al Burro e Salvia

Ingredients:

- 400 g (14 oz) ricotta ravioli (store-bought or homemade)
- 1/4 cup unsalted butter
- 10 fresh sage leaves
- Salt and pepper, to taste
- Grated Parmesan cheese, for serving

Instructions:

1. **Cook the Ravioli**
   Boil salted water and cook ravioli according to package instructions.
2. **Prepare the Sauce**
   In a skillet, melt butter over medium heat. Add sage leaves and cook until fragrant.
3. **Combine Ravioli and Sauce**
   Drain ravioli and add to the skillet, tossing to coat in the sage butter.
4. **Serve**
   Season with salt and pepper, and sprinkle with grated Parmesan before serving.

Fettuccine alla Ricotta

Ingredients:

- 400 g (14 oz) fettuccine
- 1 cup ricotta cheese
- 1/2 cup grated Parmesan cheese
- 1/4 cup olive oil
- Salt and pepper, to taste
- Fresh parsley, for garnish

Instructions:

1. **Cook the Pasta**
   Boil a large pot of salted water and cook fettuccine until al dente.
2. **Prepare the Sauce**
   In a bowl, mix ricotta, Parmesan, olive oil, salt, and pepper until smooth.
3. **Combine Pasta and Sauce**
   Drain fettuccine and toss with the ricotta sauce until well coated.
4. **Serve**
   Garnish with fresh parsley before serving.

Printed in the USA
CPSIA information can be obtained
at www.ICGtesting.com
LVHW080715041124
795620LV00004B/16